T0381215

CHRONICLES
OF
CAROLS IN COLOR

THE STORYBOOK

JAYE ALLISON

AuthorHouse™
1663 Liberty Drive
Bloomington, IN 47403
www.authorhouse.com
Phone: 1 (800) 839-8640

Published by AuthorHouse 12/09/2015

ISBN: 978-1-5049-6448-7 (sc)
ISBN: 978-1-5049-6447-0 (e)

Author, Jaye Allison
Images from Jaye Allison's photographic archives
Additional images illustrated by Orah Stanish
Author's Biographical photograph by Mitch Martinez

Permissions for Periodicals granted by: Irv Randolph, Managing Editor of The Philadelphia Tribune articles June 9, 1981 and December 31,1985
Thank you Nancy Goldner, Dance Critic, AuthorSusan Gould for The Philadelphia Inquirer quotes circa 1991-95Deni Kasrel for The Philadelphia
Inquirer quotes circa 1991-95Merilyn Jackson for The Philadelphia Inquirer quotes circa 1992-95Madeline Schrock and Brenda Dixon-
Gottschild, Ph.D.Prof. Emerita, Temple University for Dance Magazine quotes circa 1992-94C. S'thembile West, Ph.D., Professor Emerita,
Western Illinois University for the Philadelphia Inquirer quote December 1994 and The Philadelphia Weekly March 29, 1995 Feature Article

Print information available on the last page.

CONTENTS

Book Description

The Chronicles of Carols In Color by: Jaye Allison

It is my sincere hope, sharing part of my testimony can encourage youths of all ages through this personal "How To" follow your dream diagram, told in storybook form.

Pursuing a dance career on your own is the story painted in this historical document. This testimony of my childhood dream to become a dance artist is very personal and I believe you can get something out of it. Coming from J. P. Turner Middle School, dancing in the Big Musical 'Dreamland Cafe' and a friend teaching me ballet in her basement, there was catching up to do as I auditioned and made a place in the brand new performing arts magnet high school to begin serious training. It was there I met my dancing soul mate and found some local notoriety producing and co-directing a dance company since turning 18. This relationship, which led to creating a Philadelphia area annual Christmas holiday tradition was 17 years in the making.

Thank You, you lovely people:

My Mother Phyllis and Grandmother Dorothy for helping me find me so many years ago with no judgements, through the fog. Siblings, Walter Jr. for sketching the 1st artistic rendering and Iris for creating the 1st edits. You kicked off my 1st book offering and gave this effort the best start a little sister could ask!

All of the T-Shirt fund raising contributors to the process that encouraged this idea. You know who you are to me and I am always proud to call you friends and artistic supporters!

Chris Burbage, contributions come in more forms than money and because of yours this package is complete!

JAYE ALLISON

LEON EVANS

Dedicated to... all the youthful dance dreamers; may your dreams become the reality you see. To the memories of: my lil' Sis in dance, Toni Marie Chalmers Lombre, Founder of Taps & Company (DC) and to my partner in crime (LaVaughn Robinson called us that nickname all the time) Edward Leon Evans, Co-Founder of LEJA DANCE THEATRE. Both, gone way too soon and their dance voices are truly inspiring and deeply missed. They helped this world by making dance champions and stars shine. The deceased or missing company members that helped build LEJA's reputation 1983- 86: William Whit!eld Jr., Darren 'Tonka' Mears, Shirley Myles, Amos 'Buster' Moore, Mark Davis and a few more beautiful people who loved every good and special thing about dance. Bravissimo!! To their Shining Stars, legacies and incredible unsung moments.

Forewords

Cheryl Hazzard, Maurice Hines Jr., Joan Huckstep & Susan Glazer

This is is an exciting, practical and awesome book that takes you through a little girls dreams, visions and journey as she grows and develops her talents. The book shares her experiences in how she ran into obstacles but implemented problem solving skills to help resolve those issues. So many of our youth need to read this book to realize that they too can achieve their dreams.

I first had Jaye and her siblings during my first assignment as a new Music Teacher and Department Head at the Turner Middle School. At that time there was full funding for the Creative Arts within the School District of Philadelphia which provided many opportunities and experiences for young students to explore and develop their creative talents. All students in the school had at least one period of music each week. Choir, Instrumental, piano, organ lessons, and ensembles were available for students. Here, Jaye learned music history, theory and vocal techniques as well as having the opportunity to perform in the classroom and assemblies. She was chosen to sing in the District One Choir where music teachers in each district selected talented students to participate by performing every year in a large festival. At Turner Middle School, 8th Grade English Teacher, Barry Gordon, who was knowledgeable about musicals, helped collaborate with the Music Department to produce the school's first musical that ended up touring in close vicinity. Jaye auditioned and was selected to dance the solo role in the Cab Calloway feature 'Minnie the Moocher'. We were amazed at how it all came together. The high number of talented students in this school made and created a successful venture that broadened optimism to the point that former students still rely on information from their Turner School experiences to compare with life today. It is reassuring to see that Jaye has groomed so many students in the field of Dance, demonstrating and guiding the careers of many lives leading to outstanding results.

I am so happy to have been a part of the picture used by God as a vessel to encourage Jaye to discover her abilities and God given gifts. I am proud of her creativity, dedication and perseverance.

Cheryl M. Hazzard, BM, BME, M.Ed.

Phila. Tribune
June 9, 1981

MU CHAPTER of Gamma Phi Delta Sorority, Inc., recently presented Jaye Lynne Allison, "Artist of Tomorrow," at the Eugene Wayman Jones Cultural Center, 5148 Walnut St. In the group are (from left) Soror Olivia Turner, program coordinator; Derrick Lott, speaker; Jaye Lynne Allison, the artist; Soror Sara B. Young, chairman, and Soror Juanita Watkins.—Wm. A. Byrd photo

To say LEON EVANS was the most talented man I ever met would be the ultimate understatement of my life . I met LEON when we both were chosen to hit broadway in BRING BACK BIRDY starring the great CHITA RIVERA, from the first day of rehearsal watching him dance it was clear to me I was in the presence of greatness. His versatility was nothing short of astounding but as wonderful as that was it was LEON'S big heart for everyone that came within his world that will always set him apart . He was a truly wonderful person. There will never ever be another LEON EVANS and I will always be grateful that God put him on this earth for all of us to love and forever be inspired by . Love You Always.

Maurice Hines Jr.

Dec 16, 1985 to Jan 11, 1986
Forrest Theatre

Dec 31, 1985.

RAMSEY

Continued from Page 25

shaped like a jungle princess gonna wear people out."

Evans is talking about Delp Mantz, 29, a fellow student Philadelphia College of the Pe ing Arts. Big hipped. Th thighed. An outrageously fii per.

She does two flips that caus ble gasps in the audience.

She says stuff like, "I don't l many slow-paced things. I'm vibrant."

Her vibrancy is confirmed Chanze Sapp — a thin, big-voi year-old, PCPA-trained vocali sings the Marvelettish lead on Mess With Bill" and is Mantz friend.

"Her giggle," Sapp says ecstr ly. "Her honesty. Her spe Ummmm …"

The "Uptown" Philadelphi tingent is rounded out by people Toni-Maria Chalmers, anna Graves, Lisa Ann Mallo Elise Neal. The idea is slowly ing on all of them that Broadw moved from a world away t over the next hill. Where it i ing for them in mid-January.

"Last year," Sapp says in lously, "I was working at Th lery. Making $3.45 an hour. month, I'll be singing on Bro It's like wow! It's like whew! I v shine, shine, shine … "

If You Go

Marion Ramsey and her sev low-Philadelphians star with rice Hines in pre-Broadway "Uptown … It's Hot!" at the F Theatre, 1114 Walnut St. The has been extended through J Box Office: 923-1515.

Staff Photography by G. Lois Grossmann —

The Philadelphia contingent in "Uptown . . . It's Hot!" includes (atop couch, from left) Ruthanna Graves, Elise Neal, Delphine T. Mantz, R. LaChanze Sapp and Lisa Ann Mallory; and (seated) Leon Evans and Marion Ramsey

I met Leon Evans while choreographing a production of Amen Corner at the now defunct Theatre Center of Philadelphia who was the music director. I could tell from his walk that he was a dancer and spoke to him immediately about dancing in the production and working together on some independent productions. He smiled and said "we'll talk." A few days later, we met and he brought Jaye Allison with him. Although both of them were still in high school; it was obvious that they were a creative pair—quite a formidable creative pair at that. Even at that young age they were compositionally sophisticated producing works and finding performance outlets. We worked together for many years (1981-through 1996) when the company dissolved each going their separate ways.

Theirs was more than a creative partnership; it was a creative marriage. Over those years, I was a first hand observer of their process. While each was a gifted choreographer in his/her own right, often they co-created works seamlessly beginning and finishing choreographic thoughts. They shared administrative responsibilities marketing, venue negotiation, box office set up, fundraising, and production costume and lighting design, stage/rehearsal management. Both were competent and assumed these various roles and responsibilities as their individual circumstances of time and resources dictated. Both became respected members of the Philadelphia dance community collectively and individually.

As their lives progressed each pursued personal opportunities for growth that took them out of Philadelphia. Jaye spent a fruitful stint in Italy where she returned with even more mature choreographic strengths. 1990 'Il Viaggio a Shangrilah' 1991 'Con Piacere', 'Twisted Fate' on Philadanco members. It further imbued through the popular Black Jazz 101- Skidelybop and 'Carols in Color'. Leon was on the road a lot with Bowser's Rock and Roll production. They began moving through the upper echelons of the dance world beyond Philadelphia. Jaye cultivated a relationship with Rod Rodgers in New York who set a work on LEJA. Jaye worked tirelessly to secure the grant for that production and managed the rehearsals and dancers.

As often happens, as they grew individually their "marriage" began to unravel. We began a six-month project during which I was the company administrator trying to sort out the issues. In a letter to Charon Battles of the Pennsylvania Council on the Arts I wrote:

'We will be working on developing an organizational structure (including obtaining 501C3 status), and a marketing/fundraising strategy that is more suited to where LEJA is and needs today. We already have several consultant resource people already working with LEJA (in particular Rod Rodgers who not only has set a work on the company but has provided invaluable time and guidance on many arts administration matters). We have also been talking with Ann Edmonds [an arts administrative consultant par excellent] and are currently in the middle of working out an agreement for her to work with LEJA.'

Keeping their company together became impossible and the company formally dissolved in the spring of 1995. The "divorce" was painful for each of them. In a letter to them both, I wrote:

'While the going of separate ways may be difficult at the present moment, I believe that in the long run this has the possibility of being a positive turning point for more successful future endeavors for both of you.'

It is more often than not it is sad to see a breakup of a longstanding marriage—creative or otherwise. However, often it is the products of the partnership that survive and thrive to delight people well after the breakup. This is the case with LEJA—the Leon Evans Jaye Allison union. In particular is the case of their seminal work Carols in Color which has been in annual production since its inception now produced by Leon's company Eleone. This book is another continuation of their creative product. Jaye has put forth an invaluable road map for young independent artists on the quest of realizing their creative vision and a teaching aid for dance educators helping their students to learn the means of mounting a production without the traditional resources.

Dr. Joan Huckstep

Jaye Allison and Leon Evans, Leja Dance Theatre

As the Director of the School of Dance of the University of the Arts for 30 years, I had the pleasure to work with Jaye and Leon when they were both undergraduate students in Dance back in the 1980's. As part of my position, I worked with literally hundreds of aspiring professional dancers, choreographers and teachers. It is, and was at the time, abundantly clear that these two young artists had the passion, vision and energy to make a difference in dance – to create a company and a body of work that would be long lasting and important to the community. There are a few students whose contributions to the school have stayed with me for years. Jaye and Leon are two of the best. Leon's untimely passing made it even more compelling for Jaye to assure the continuation of the work and she has done an outstanding job.

Their "Carols in Color" has become their most notable and frequently presented work, surpassing even their signature, "Oluwa," and has become a standard of excellence in dance performance. The University of the Arts is proud to call them alumni.

Susan Glazer

Chapter 1 - 1978

18 years old: Our First publicity shot as Co-Directors and Original Logo both handcrafted by Leon during Winter of 1982

Once, there was a Black Dance company named LEJA DANCE THEATRE, founded by Leon Evans and Jaye Allison.

They had been in love with each other's dance styles ever since they met in Center City at the Philadelphia High School for the Creative and Performing Arts, Fall of 1978. Leon was the new high school's bona fide Broadway Star who wasted little time showing what it meant! And without hesitation, started to organize after school rehearsals, gathering 14-18 dance classmates to learn choreography and to see how far he could take it. Each dancer came from somewhere in Philadelphia, and those were the places this group, 'The Company with Class Dancers' performed!

From the beginning, they had great teachers who helped them mold their techniques in all forms of dance: Classical Ballet - Cecchetti, Vaganova and American, Modern techniques of Horton, Limon, Duncan and Improvisation, Theater Dance with Broadway Jazz and Tap, Ethnic Studies of Dunham and Liturgical and yes, there were more. This high octane training developed their individual skillsets and permanently molded their signature styles. Yet they always trained with a yearning and desire to learn more and more...

4 years later, one week after graduation, summer of 1982 to be exact. They continued the troupe but needed a new name to keep it going. Leon wanted something unique and classic. He thought of a few ways to fancy up his name, Le Danse, Elle' Danse, Eleone and others but he didn't get great responses from Jaye. So he thought, and thought until he spoke up saying "Lay-Zhah".

Asking Jaye what she thought, she said "Oo~la~la! It sounds French and memorable… umm, but what does it mean, like, what is it?!" He said proudly, "It's our initials!" Jaye hollered loudly and laughed full bellied, replying "that is so clever! It's perfect! It's us!"

Leon and Jaye reformed the dance group with 4 members and was ushered into the world of professional concert dance by their high school's Modern Dance teacher. She felt her students were ready to represent a future of the Horton legacy passed down from Philadelphia's Horton Dance Master, Joan Kerr, who passed away in January that year. The Painted Bride Arts Center was the stage where all the dance companies and soloists touched by her life's work gathered to pay public tribute. The group performed 'Oluwa - Many Rains Ago'. It made quite the impression and became the group's Signature work.

LEJA quickly doubled in size within its 1st year! Mainly because Jaye entered the Philadelphia College of Performing Arts that September, followed by Leon in January. The wealth of technically sound dancers found in this world famous Dance Department was beyond compare!

It was funny to see the faces of people, especially Emcees, mispronounce the company name… Leeha, Layha, LeeJay…. It was several years before people learned the correct pronunciation.

Signature work:
Oluwa 1981

They danced on lots of stages! LEJA was the first dance group Six Flags Great Adventures Amusement Park invited to showcase local dance artists in 1985. They also performed...

on television, in night clubs, birthdays and weddings.

"Baby, I'm a Star!" - 1984

In plays and at outdoor festivals. Any and every place they could, LEJA DANCE THEATRE did!

They even doubled their identity as the Power 99FM Dancers 1983-86. The new black radio station's reputation gained face value with publicity campaigns using Hot Jazz dancers alongside tv ads showcasing a silhouette dancer appearing throughout the Philadelphia metropolitan area: store openings, car washes, 3 yearly PowerHouse dance parties and always in nightclubs as far as Atlantic City!

LEON EVANS & JAYE ALLISON
CLASS OF '62
RETURN TO PERFORM A BENEFIT CONCERT

FOR CAPA'S PROFESSIONAL INSTRUCTION
FUND with the dance company they
both founded here at CAPA...

IN CONCERT!!
MARCH 6 1987 8pm Curtain
Phila. High School for Creative and
Performing Arts -- 11th & Catherine
Street -- in their fine auditorium
ADMISSION $5.00

Please support CAPA's veteran talent,
a worthy cause and one of the HOTTEST
Young companies Philly has to offer

Chapter 2
The Next Level

With much hype around the region about the dance company, gigs almost doubled, as did the bills! This is an expected concern. Mother Nature demanded LEJA give birth to the grassrooted efforts taking them from the 'Street Theater' to the permanent concert stage level! Looks like it is time for the directors dreaming and training to be put to the test…

Leon always liked the idea of booty bumpin' music, good food and a piano around to make sure his soulful, touching vocals can add that unique, magical touch into everyone at once! That was his way of saying "Thank you!". His ideas and locations never failed to please. Fundraiser parties were held and lots of raffle tickets were sold, all in an effort to raise money to keep the company alive.

When the directors' pockets were empty, being a small troupe with big dreams, LEJA needed a means for more extensive advertising and booking opportunities. Print and radio was how most people get their news so it was time to go in that direction. It's time for some press reviews.

All the major and local press was invited to their home season concert series at Community College of Philadelphia. Leon said every place a LEJA dancer lives is a neighborhood newspaper needing to report what the people around them are doing. "I'll make the press release and send them to all their papers and the big name papers too!"

They prepared to 'wow' the critics and had butterflies and jitters awaiting to hear the ushers report on their reactions to the company's 'Feel the Fire- Spirited- Social Justice themed- Passionate' dance suites! The company danced long and hard those 2 evenings.

Takin' it to the Streets, the suite- part 2 -1985

jumping high and serving draaamaa with the technical skills they are well known for! OH, YUSS!! Snap in a Z formation kind of performance!!... to their disappointment, the directors learned 2 out of 12 personally invited newspaper staff members attended, and 1 even took notes!

"Well, at least the neighborhood press appeared!" Jaye said to Leon in a quiet moment. This small step didn't change for 2 more seasons. What was the problem? Everyone loves LEJA. Right?

Leon and Jaye called on their board of directors for answers. They made phone calls and came back with little to share on the subject. Jaye decided to call on a few local show producers and their advice was "move to a reviewable venue". In other words, a marketable place that is an established theater where people are used to going. This was going to call for a bigger budget! Jaye told the board all about it and Leon got more contract jobs to help.

Spring 1992… Timing is everything!! As it happens, there was movement to open new theater opportunities for small dance companies like LEJA and they jumped at it! Problem Solved! It worked! Movement Theater International's DANCE NOW! Collaborative Concert Series received $152,500 in total grant money to keep the dance community thriving!

CHAPTER 3
THE LIGHTBULB
MOMENT

How the
Star
Appeared

Having reached that goal, enjoying the benefits and soon after the Spring of '92 Concerts, Leon and Jaye were eating dinner when he mentioned how tired he had been of helping with and seeing the dance world stop during the winter for THE NUTCRACKER. Jaye agreed by asking "Why isn't there a traditional Black Christmas Dance show?". "We need options!" said Leon.

"We should make history and do one", says Jaye "I'm already thinking of ideas" replied Leon "How does 'Charlie Dark Brown' sound?" "'Happy' is already choreographed from the circus!" It was a great idea. Jaye loved the thought of creating black Peanuts dancing characters! Leon also thought of the Black Nutcracker, but Jaye insisted that idea would not change anyone's mind by saying "Hasn't that already been done?!..." Leon remembered something. "... I've heard of a play that had roots in North Philadelphia by Langston Hughes, named Black Nativity. It premiered in the 1960's and ran annually for a while." Turning to look at his partner in crime with an evil grin, "It has not been seen in decades! It was the story of Jesus' birth, casting people of color in every role, because everybody knows Jesus was a man of color! His description is in the Bible."

"OOOHH! This is Biblical Theatre that can be danced!" Jaye liked this idea best of all! She wanted to know more. Leon had only heard of the theatrical legacy but knew he would be going to work in Washington, DC soon with theatre friends and knew where he could get a copy of the script! They had found a new goal, creating a new traditional Black Christmas Dance show.

By the end of May, Leon finished working in Washington, DC and returned with what he had promised. Jaye asked to see the script but he never pulled it out except to show her that he had it. His face was not happy. He said he was disappointed because it was only script in the first half, but after intermission, it's all singing!

Leon finally took a deep breath to speak, saying "if that's the case, we need to write our own script" walking over to his big family bible on the coffee table and opened it to St. Matthew and handed it to Jaye saying, "everything is here that we need, I like his version the best…", referring to the Gospel according to Matthew. Jaye grew up in church as well, and knew this was true.

Now, after pulling together a script outline that suited their ideas and as they scheduled summer rehearsals for the group, Leon worked to gather his musical groups and soloists. His contacts were vast, internationally recognized performers alongside up-and-coming local performing artists. He also owned an artist development company that finally used another of the brand names thought of years ago ~ Eleone!

LEON AND JAYE HAD A LOT OF WORK TO DO!
THEY HAPPILY SAT DOWN TO PUT TOGETHER THE NUTS AND BOLTS OF THE NEW PROJECT BASED ON
THE BIBLICAL NATIVITY, USING THEIR FAVORITE CHRISTMAS CAROLS, ARRANGED BY LEON OF COURSE!
THEY DID NOT STOP UNTIL THE EARLY MORNING.

BRAINSTORMING, THEY DECIDED ON THE OVERALL STAGING CONCEPT
AND WHAT WOULD BE NEEDED TO PULL IT TOGETHER:

MARY AND JOSEPH AND THEIR ANGELS
SINGING IN A STYLE LIKE CECE & BEBE WINANS

MARY'S PREGNANCY
CHANGING TO SHOW THE
PASSAGE OF TIME, THE
INNKEEPER, A LA 'MAHALIA
JACKSON' TO ANNOUNCE
THE BIRTH OF JESUS

DANCE THE
INNOCENCE—

DANCE IN
HEAVENLY PEACE—

DANCE THE
CONFUSION—

DANCE IN HEAVENLY
CELEBRATION. JESUS IS BORN—

DANCE IN PRAISE.
FINI...

AND WITH A LITTLE PURPOSEFUL
WORD PLAY, THEY CAME UP WITH:

CAROLS
IN COLOR

PRACTICALLY SAYING IT AT THE SAME
TIME, LAUGHING AND FIGHTING OVER
WHO SAID IT FIRST!

CHAPTER 4

1992

14 years Later…

A "reviewable theater" was chosen. A place audiences were already used to going. Movement Theater International was not only the 1st Theater offering LEJA opportunities for advancement, but it was housed in a Historic Landmark Church built in 1886 complete with overhead seating that would suit the inspired church/ processional choir and dancer idea. It was perfect!

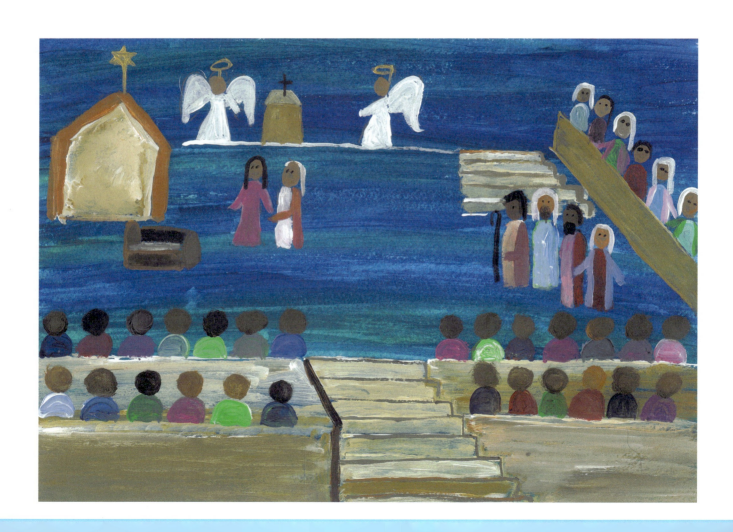

It was a memorable summer with things developing quickly and the dance world was all a BUZZ! LEJA DANCE THEATRE is trying to compete with the NUTCRACKER!

There was lots of love, support and energy from every dancer, singer, manager, board member, crew, family, friends and strangers. This production felt like a success, even before the first curtain!

With Carols in Color cast and crew rehearsed as much as possible, only last minute details remained. Leon and Jaye will dance the solos as the Angels for Mary & Joseph.

On that day, they finally found the perfect songs for their roles - *the lead male vocalist flew in from out of town and had beautiful suggestions...* 'I'll be With You' and 'Faith that Conquers Anything', inspired their staging and choreographic imagery just as theater rehearsals began.

The other small detail Jaye insisted on was a different kind of intermission marker, saying to him… "You know what? Instead of the usual announcement or flickering lights, let's wake up everyone with the sound of a baby crying and laughing! That can be the signal! "THE BABY JESUS IS BORN", hurry! Come see for yourselves!!" Leon smiled and said, "I got this". Then left the building to make it happen…

Leon and Jaye led the anxious group with fearless confidence. Opening Nite has arrived!! Wow!! So many people, the theater was oversold, pushing even the standing room only audience members past capacity! To the company's joy, this outstanding attendance continued throughout the 3 day 4 show run which ended Christmas Eve at Midnight!!

Not a single audience member complained!!! They loved the idea of beginning Christmas in a church celebrating the "Highest Reason for the Season!!"

The road to becoming a tradition has just begun. It takes 3 consecutive successful annual runs before being legitimately able to use and earn that label! Leon and Jaye were very aware of how long it took for people to pronounce 'LEJA' and this popularity must spread by a fierce reputation. Well, the tv and newspaper articles "RAVED". Now they are prepared for year 2!

Jaye learned how to keep the company's dreams going by writing grants. She found out that Pennsylvania's Council on the Arts helped new companies become stable and made sure she met the director of the correct program department for guidance.

Year 2…

The dancer pool grew to 21 incredible performers, and the singers never sounded better and more wonderful reviews rolled in…

"When was the last time you saw a stage about the sacred birth of baby Jesus at which the audience hooted as though they were at a sports event" -Philadelphia Inquirer, Deni Kasrel

"T'was a cold winter's night, when visions of joy to the world danced in the air…to a packed house on a Wednesday opening night" Dance Magazine, Brenda Dixon

Hallelujah Chorus 1992

"Carols in Color is a non-stop ode to joy" – Philadelphia Inquirer, Susan Gould

Year 3...

The cast was trimmed and a proper stage set (easy to assemble) for touring the show was bought. And then that magical time happened!! Great reviews continued, sold out houses that overflowed with the unique Christmas Eve 10:30pm showing.

".. in addition to being solemn, Carols is slammin'" Philadelphia Inquirer, Merilyn Jackson

"This rendition of the nativity is TOTAL THEATER" - Dance Magazine, Brenda Dixon

"Carols in Color...is an area tradition" - Philadelphia Inquirer, C. S'thembile West

"This praise-dance-based company nourishes performers...and new audiences for them" – Philadelphia Inquirer, Deni Kasrel

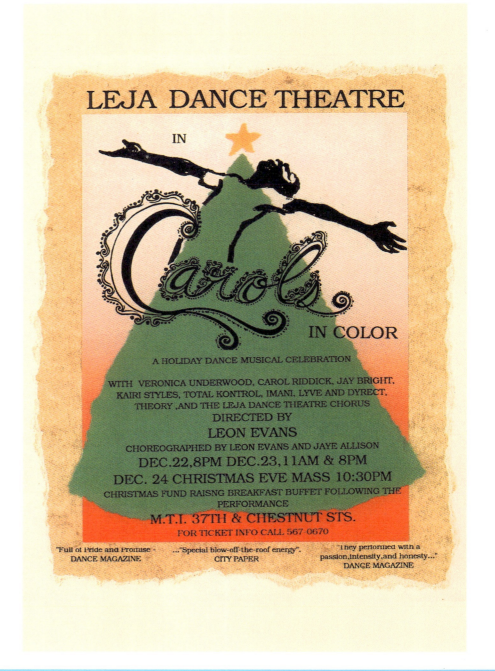

LEJA DANCE THEATRE
IN

Carols
IN COLOR

A HOLIDAY DANCE MUSICAL CELEBRATION

WITH VERONICA UNDERWOOD, CAROL RIDDICK, JAY BRIGHT, KAIRI STYLES, TOTAL KONTROL, IMANI, LYVE AND DYRECT, THEORY ,AND THE LEJA DANCE THEATRE CHORUS
DIRECTED BY
LEON EVANS
CHOREOGRAPHED BY LEON EVANS AND JAYE ALLISON
DEC.22,8PM DEC.23,11AM & 8PM
DEC. 24 CHRISTMAS EVE MASS 10:30PM
CHRISTMAS FUND RAISNG BREAKFAST BUFFET FOLLOWING THE PERFORMANCE
M.T.I. 37TH & CHESTNUT STS.
FOR TICKET INFO CALL 567-0670

"Full of Pride and Promise -
DANCE MAGAZINE

..."Special blow-off-the-roof energy".
CITY PAPER

They performed with a
passion,intensity,and honesty..."
DANCE MAGAZINE

Leon and Jaye finally celebrated together, privately, eventually, as usual... and planned to enjoy the new Black Dance Historical imprint made in the artistic fabric of Philadelphia's Christmas Tapestry.

Except, it is January. 9 weeks until the 15th Anniversary Spring 1995 Concert Season hits the stage!

LEJA

DANCE THEATRE
15TH ANNIVERSARY
1980 - 1995
"CELEBRATION"

4 DIFFERENT EVENINGS CELEBRATING 15 YEARS OF EXCELLENCE

ROD ROGERS' "QUEST"
MELVIN PURNELL'S "THE SEDUCTION OF SHANGO AND OSHUN"
RAYMOND HARRIS "REACHING UP FROM THE BOTTOM"
"CHARLIE DARK BROWN" (HAPPY)
"BIRDLAND"
SHAWN LAMERE'S "THE QUESTION IS..."
"CON PIACERE"
"HALLELUJAH" FROM CAROLS IN COLOR

SAT. MARCH 25 SPECIAL GUEST COMPANY RENNIE HARRIS' PURE MEOVEMENT

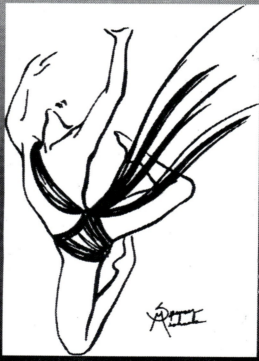

"LEJA DANCE THEATRE exudes joy"-

Susan Gould
City Paper

"They performed with a passion, intensity, and honesty."

Brenda Dixon
Dance Magazine

"Joy is exactly what the company delivers"

Nancy Goldner
Philadelphia Inquirer

MARCH 22-25
MOVEMENT THEATRE INTERNATIONAL
3700 CHESTNUT ST.
UPSTAGES BOX OFFICE 893-1145

Yes, this professional relationship lasted 17 extraordinary years, culminating with the creation of a new Christmas tradition, CAROLS IN COLOR!!! Things are looking up! Grants from the state and other funding sources have brought in a total of $70,000 to LEJA DANCE THEATRE for its 16th season.

Black Jazz
101-Skidelybop
aka Birdland
1991

Leon and Jaye were grateful
and both continued teaching,
sharing, developing hundreds
of artists, touching lives
and believing in Jesus
to make a difference.

They were making
their mark and
the arts have
spread farther
and wider with
the LEJA spirit.

NOT EVERYONE
LOVES THE NUTCRACKER
And the LEJA Dance Theatre knows it.

BY C. S'THEMBILE WEST

Homegrown visionaries Leon Evans and Jaye Allison have enriched artistic life in Philadelphia for 15 years. In celebration of those years, the **LEJA Dance Theatre** performed at Movement Theater International last week.

LEJA (which stands for the co-founders' first initials), celebrates Philadelphia. Perhaps their most moving event has been **Carols in Color**, a reenactment of the story of the nativity told African-American style. Complete with gospel music and interpretive liturgy, *Carols* is billed as an alternative to *The Nutcracker*, an ageless ballet from European classical dance circa 1890's.

Despite the mass appeal of *The Nutcracker* among balletomanes, it does not always reach and/or inspire children and adults from inner-city environments. Hence, *Carols in Color* was created to reach those who might prefer Langston Hughes' *Black Nativity*, which inspired the making of *Carols in Color*.

LEJA Dance Theatre's *Carols in Color*, directed by Leon Evans and jointly choreographed with Jaye Allison, has been presented in Philadelphia for three seasons. The beauty of *Carols in Color* can be found in its dramatic flair and simple elegance. The dancers have the kind of spirit and energy that oozes past the stage lights and touches people in their seats. LEJA dancers display pizzazz, stamina and joy that transforms and defies common gestures. *Carols in Color* has repeatedly been a rousing success in Philadelphia as well as the Christina Arts Center in Wilmington, Delaware this past holiday season.

However, what underlies the success of LEJA resonates in the lives, philosophy and ongoing commitment of its founders. When they met, Evans and Allison were mere teenagers studying dance at the Philadelphia School of the Creative and Performing Arts

(CAPA). As members of CAPA's first class, they found each other and built a company foundation with the skills they had honed there.

When Allison was in the second grade, she shared the excitement of dance with her best friend Michelle, who attended the Massey School of Dance at 69th and Market Sts. in Upper Darby, and who had performed in a recital at the Academy of Music. About that experience, Allison recalled: "I had never seen a theater before. And we had orchestra seats.

We were center left. I wore my lace cinnamon dress with a ribbon around it. I was sitting with Michelle's mom, Miss Diane. I was looking at the large chandeliers. A guy came out with a top hat and you could see his glow-in-the-dark tap shoes. You could only see feet, hands and a glow… I had never seen that before. If you have never seen it, then you don't know what it is. That was the moment I had started paying attention to dance."

Her focus never let up, and she continually bugged her mother about going to dancing school-a dream that went unfulfilled at that time, "because," says Allison, "being a second grader, I didn't understand economics." Her opportunity came when she entered CAPA. There she learned modern dance technique and at the same time attended the Massey School of Dance.

Upon graduation in 1982, Jaye Allison and Leon Evans were the only members of the CAPA dance crew known as The Company with Class Dancers, and they became LEJA "out of that friendship which we honed in high school," Allison Emphasizes.

That same year, they landed a gig to dance for Power 99 FM. "With the addition of Danco members, the quality of dancers increased." recalls Evans.

Perhaps LEJA would not have been formed if Danco wasn't going through changes. By the time LEJA was formed, Evans had been in rehearsal for a show in New York. He'd received high school materials on Monday (via correspondence school),

go home on Friday mornings for tests, then, return to NY by seven to make a seven-thirty curtain at the Martin Beck Theater for *Bring Back Birdie* with Chita Rivera, Donald O'Conner and Maurice Hines. LEJA Dance Theatre is not only a creative vehicle for Allison and Evans; they have specific ideas about why they do what they do. Says Evans: "The connection between the dancers and the audience is most important to keep people who are not artists in the theater." Both believe that dance changes people's lives. "I think that we as artists in the theater can have an effect on people," says Evans, who attended University of the Arts in 1984 so that he could make a difference in the school system. "I can see not only the difference the arts made in the educational process, but the difference it made in their own lives. And because of my connection with my family, I can see both sides of the fence. Poverty is key."

He continues, "I just wish that parents of children would just support and love… just support an interest. But you can't do that if you don't have no money. Our art will only succeed if my kids from North Philadelphia can see it, they will go out and get a job so they can pay for a ticket to see. They will spend the money that they do have on things that are important to them."

Allison's vision for LEJA is also deeply rooted in community. She sees LEJA as a conduit "to feed the community of African-Americans in Philadelphia."

As was evident Wednesday through Saturday performances last week at Movement Theater International, LEJA Dance Theatre attracts dancers who work hard to keep the truth about dance alive in Philadelphia. After 15 years LEJA consistently brings vibrancy to the Philadelphia arts community. More importantly, according to Allison, "they are there because they love what they do."

He will always live on in
my heart… 1964-1998

Printed in the United States
By Bookmasters